Timothy Training Program

STUDENTS MANUAL

*Equipping Leaders
for the Twenty-first
Century Church*

Copyright © 1994
Frank Damazio
Portland, Oregon

ISBN# 0-914936-13-1

Available from:

CITYBIBLE
PUBLISHING

9200 NE FREMONT • PORTLAND, OR 97220
PHONE 1-800-777-6057• FAX 503-257-2228
www.citybiblepublishing.com • E-MAIL: equip@citybiblepublishing.com

Published by City Bible Publishing
9200 NE Fremont
Portland, Oregon 97220

Printed in U.S.A.

City Bible Publishing is a ministry of City Bible Church and is dedicated to serving the local church and its leaders through the production and distribution of quality restoration materials.

It is our prayer that these materials, proven in the context of the local church, will equip leaders in exalting the Lord and extending His kingdom.

For a free catalog of additional resources from City Bible Publishing please call 1-800-777-6057 or visit our web site at www.citybiblepublishing.com.

Timothy Training Program – Student's Manual
© Copyright 1994 by City Bible Publishing
All Rights Reserved

ISBN 0-914936-13-1

Timothy Training Program
Table of Contents

THE LIFE OF TIMOTHY

PROGRESS
The Perseverance
Factor
(I Tim 4:15)

PERSPECTIVE
Finishing Strong
(II Tim 4)

PLACEMENT
The Responsibility
Trust
(Acts 20; I Tim 1:3)

Local Church Overseer

(II Tim 1-4)

PROMOTION
The Revealer
(II Tim 4:6)

CHOOSING
The Selection
(Acts 16)

Local Church Preparation | Local Church Leadership

(Acts 16; I Tim 1-6)

EQUIPPING
The Impartation
(Acts 13-15,18
II Tim 3:10-12)

(Acts 14,16)

INVITATION
The Calling
(Mt 22)

RESPONSE
The Power of Choice
(Acts 14)

Timothy Training Program
Requirements and Expectations

◆ **Requirements**

- Please commit yourself to the total package. This means both husband and wife must attend <u>all</u> sessions together.

- It is necessary for the wife to be as committed as the husband for all training sessions. This is a team focused program.

- Please bring your Bible. At the first class you will be given a Timothy Training Program notebook.

- Please come at least five to ten minutes prior to the starting time. We will start promptly according to our schedule.

- Dress is casual.

◆ **Expectations**

- You will be expected to pray, worship and enter into the discussions. Everybody should come prepared spiritually to give.

- You are being trained to be a leader. Come with an attitude of teachableness.

- You will be personally prayed for by the class during our time together.

- By the end of the class we fully expect you to take a significant leadership role in serving this local church.

◆ **Supplemental Reading**

- <u>The Making of a Leader</u> by Frank Damazio
- <u>Effective Keys to Successful Leadership</u> by Frank Damazio
- <u>The Vanguard Leader</u> by Frank Damazio

Timothy Training Program
Teaching Sessions

	Introduction to the Timothy Program	• Hand out Timothy Training Notebook • Hand out dates, times, place • Hand out requirements, expectations and guidelines • Hand out your local church vision statement
#1	**Introduction to the Life of Timothy: The Invitation**	• Go over the chart • Teach on "Calling: The Invitation" • Personal sharing: God is inviting me to...?
#2	**Life of Timothy: The Response**	• Go over the chart • Teach on heart conditions and excuses • Discuss personal obstacles and right excuses
#3	**Local Church Proving and Preparation I**	• Teach on planting, discipling and personal problems • Discuss what it means to be planted • Teach on being proven and submissive attitudes
#4	**Local Church Proving and Preparation II**	• Teach on faithfulness • Discuss the main areas and why this virtue is so important • Discuss why proving is vital to protecting the church
#5	**The Choosing I: The Selection**	• Teach on the doctrine of election • Discuss the confirmations to God's choice
#6	**The Choosing II: The Character Factor**	• Teach on the character qualities from Timothy and Titus • Discuss the character qualities that fit your group
#7	**The Equipping**	• Teach on the relational foundation for equipping and ministry experiences • Discuss the difference between impartation and information • Teach on the nine things Timothy received from Paul • Discuss any of the nine areas, especially motivation and purpose
#8	**Placement**	• Teach on placement with emphasis on the pastoral charges to Timothy • Discuss and personalize some of the changes
#9	**Promotion**	• Teach on the fact and purpose of delays in God promoting leaders • Discuss the wrong concepts of promotion • Discuss and personalize these principles and deal with the ambition trap
#10	**Progress and Perseverance**	• Teach on the threats to perseverance • Discuss the personal trials you have experienced as leaders and the value of perseverance
#11	**Perspective**	• Teach on the demand for sacrifice as seen in the drink offering and the race • Discuss the leader's secret of success

x

Timothy Training Program
Session 1: The Invitation

The Life of Timothy

INVITATION The Calling (Mt 22)	CHOOSING The Selection (Acts 16)	PLACEMENT The Responsibility Trust (Acts 20; I Tim 1:3)	PROGRESS The Perseverance Factor (I Tim 4:15)
Local Church Preparation *(Acts 14,16)*	Local Church Leadership *(Acts 16; I Tim 1-6)*	Local Church Overseer *(II Tim 1-4)*	
RESPONSE The Power of Choice (Acts 14)	EQUIPPING The Impartation (Acts 13-15,18 II Tim 3:10-12)	PROMOTION The Revealer (II Tim 4:6)	PERSPECTIVE Finishing Strong (II Tim 4)

I. THE INVITATION TO ALL

    A. The Called and the Chosen, *Matthew 22:1-9, 13-14*

        1. Many Called

        2. Few Chosen

    B. The Called and the Faithful, *Revelation 17:14*

II. THOSE WHO RECEIVED INVITATION

    A. Esther, *Esther 4:14*

    B. Jeremiah, *Jeremiah 1:5*

C.   Paul, *Acts 9*

D.   David, *Acts 13*

E.   Onesimus, *Philemon 11*

F.   Demas, *II Timothy 4:10*

G.   John Mark, *II Timothy 4:11*

H.   Gideon, *Judges 6*

III.   THE INVITATION'S SPECIFIC ELEMENTS

A.   God is inviting you to live life with purpose and meaning.

Acts 13:22 "And when He had removed him, He raised up for them David as king, to whom also He gave testimony and said, 'I have found David the son of Jesse, a man after My own heart, who will do all My will.'"

B.   God is inviting you to become a tool in His hand.

Acts 9:15 But the Lord said to him, "Go, for he is a chosen vessel of Mine to bear My name before Gentiles, kings, and the children of Israel.

C.   God is inviting you to suffer for Him, bearing your cross daily.

I Peter 2:20 For what credit is it if, when you are beaten for your faults, you take it patiently? But when you do good and suffer, if you take it patiently, this is commendable before God.

D. God is inviting you to do "greater works" than Jesus did on earth.

John 14:12 Most assuredly, I say to you, he who believes in Me, the works that I do he will do also; and greater works than these he will do, because I go to My Father."

E. God is inviting you to do a specific work which only you have been called to do — "your work."

Acts 13:2 As they ministered to the Lord and fasted, the Holy Spirit said, "Now separate to Me Barnabas and Saul for the work to which I have called them."

F. God is inviting you to receive His gifting for your life.

Acts 2:38 Then Peter said to them, "Repent, and let every one of you be baptized in the name of Jesus Christ for the remission of sins; and you shall receive the gift of the Holy Spirit."

G. God is inviting you to serve. God intends you to discover where your strengths lie by serving others.

Rom 1:1 Paul, a bondservant of Jesus Christ, called to be an apostle, separated to the gospel of God.

John 13:3-5 Jesus, knowing that the Father had given all things into His hands, and that He had come from God and was going to God, rose from supper and laid aside His garments, took a towel and girded Himself. After that, He poured water into a basin and began to wash the disciples' feet, and to wipe them with the towel with which He was girded.

"Applying the Truth" Worksheet

1.   Three Insights From This Lesson

    1._____

    2._____

    3._____

2.   What I Need To Work On This Week

_____

_____

_____

_____

3.   Describe the one thing God spoke to you from this lesson.

_____

_____

_____

_____

4.   Other Comments

_____

_____

_____

_____

Timothy Training Program
Session 2: The Response

The Life of Timothy

INVITATION The Calling (Mt 22)		CHOOSING The Selection (Acts 16)		PLACEMENT The Responsibility Trust (Acts 20; I Tim 1:3)		PROGRESS The Perseverance Factor (I Tim 4:15)
	Local Church Preparation (Acts 14,16)		Local Church Leadership (Acts 16; I Tim 1-6)		Local Church Overseer (II Tim 1-4)	
RESPONSE The Power of Choice (Acts 14)		EQUIPPING The Impartation (Acts 13-15,18 II Tim 3:10-12)		PROMOTION The Revealer (II Tim 4:6)		PERSPECTIVE Finishing Strong (II Tim 4)

I.   **THE RESPONSE AND HEART CONDITION**

    A.   Importance of the Heart

        1.   Heart (Hebrew) = *labab* = whole inner life of a man: mind, will, emotions

        2.   Proverbs 4:23; Matthew 12:34-35; Mark 7:14-23

    B.   Heart Conditions

        1.   Tender

        2.   Willing

        3.   Hardened

4.   Shallow

5.   Over-crowded

6.   Embittered

II.   THE RESPONSE AND ESCAPING EXCUSES

A.   Defining The Word "Excuse"

B.   Common Unacceptable Excuses

1.   Profitable Priorities, *Luke 14:18*

2.   Reasonable Activities, *Luke 14:19*

3.   Wholesome Pleasures, *Luke 14:20*

4.   Ignoring Invitation, *Matthew 22:5*

5.   Honorable Hindrances, *Luke 9:57-62*

III. THE RIGHT RESPONSE TO GOD'S INVITATION

A. The Biblical Response

    1. Romans 12:1-2

    2. Acts 9:6

    3. Luke 1:38

    4. John 2:5

B. Your Personal Response

"Applying the Truth" Worksheet

1. Three Insights From This Lesson

    1._____

    2._____

    3._____

2. What I Need To Work On This Week

    _____

    _____

    _____

    _____

3. Describe the **one** thing God spoke to you from this lesson.

    _____

    _____

    _____

    _____

4. Other Comments

    _____

    _____

    _____

    _____

Timothy Training Program
Session 3: The Local Church Proving and Preparation, Part I

The Life of Timothy

INVITATION		CHOOSING		PLACEMENT		PROGRESS
The Calling		The Selection		The Responsibility Trust		The Perseverance Factor
(Mt 22)		(Acts 16)		(Acts 20; I Tim 1:3)		(I Tim 4:15)
	Local Church Preparation		Local Church Leadership		Local Church Overseer	
	(Acts 14,16)		(Acts 16; I Tim 1-6)		(II Tim 1-4)	
RESPONSE		EQUIPPING		PROMOTION		PERSPECTIVE
The Power of Choice		The Impartation		The Revealer		Finishing Strong
(Acts 14)		(Acts 13-15,18 II Tim 3:10-12)		(II Tim 4:6)		(II Tim 4)

I.   THE PREPARATION IN CONTEXT

A.   The Lystra Derbe Church

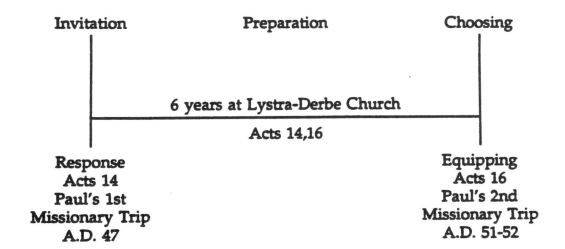

Invitation	Preparation	Choosing
	6 years at Lystra-Derbe Church	
	Acts 14,16	
Response		Equipping
Acts 14		Acts 16
Paul's 1st		Paul's 2nd
Missionary Trip		Missionary Trip
A.D. 47		A.D. 51-52

B.   Training Begins in the Local Church, Acts 16:1

1. Like a tree planted, *Psalm 1:1-4; Acts 14:21-23*

   a. Planted: Roots go deep and are fixed into the planting soil; immovable; drawing strength and nourishment and also bearing fruit to supply for others.

   b. Planted: Speaks of commitment to the local church as God's vehicle for fulfilling biblical vision, a commitment to spiritual authority and to the body of believers.

2. Like a stone placed, *I Peter 2:5-8*

C. Training Begins with a Disciple's Attitude, *Acts 16:1; 9:10,19*

D. Training Begins with Overcoming Personal Problems, *Acts 16:1*

II. THE NECESSITY OF BEING PROVEN IN THE LOCAL CHURCH

Acts 16:2 "He was well spoken of by the brethren who were at Lystra and Iconium.

   Amplified: "Timothy had a good reputation among the brethren"
   Phillips: "Timothy was held in high regard by the brethren at Lystra Iconium."

A. Good Report

1. Greek = *martureo* = to have credibility, attested, proven, approved

2. Acts 6:3; 22:12; III John 12; I Timothy 3:7; 5:10

B. **Examine the Fruit,** *I Thessalonians 5:12; I Timothy 5:16; Psalm 26:2; Exodus 16:4; 20:20; Deuteronomy 8:2; 13:3; I Thessalonians 5:21*

I Timothy 3:10 "But let these also first be proved, let them be tested, let their fruit be examined, let them undergo probation."

C. **Submissive Spirit,** *James 4:7; Hebrews 13:17; I Peter 5:5; Ephesians 5:21*

Acts 16:3 "Paul wanted to have him go on with him and he took him and circumcised him because of the Jews"

"Applying the Truth" Worksheet

1. Three Insights From This Lesson

    1._____

    2._____

    3._____

2. What I Need To Work On This Week

    _____

    _____

    _____

    _____

3. Describe the **one** thing God spoke to you from this lesson.

    _____

    _____

    _____

    _____

4. Other Comments

    _____

    _____

    _____

    _____

Timothy Training Program
Session 4: The Local Church Proving and Preparation, Part II

The Life of Timothy

INVITATION	CHOOSING	PLACEMENT	PROGRESS
The Calling	The Selection	The Responsibility Trust	The Perseverance Factor
(Mt 22)	(Acts 16)	(Acts 20; I Tim 1:3)	(I Tim 4:15)

Local Church Preparation	Local Church Leadership	Local Church Overseer
(Acts 14,16)	(Acts 16; I Tim 1-6)	(II Tim 1-4)

RESPONSE	EQUIPPING	PROMOTION	PERSPECTIVE
The Power of Choice	The Impartation	The Revealer	Finishing Strong
(Acts 14)	(Acts 13-15,18 II Tim 3:10-12)	(II Tim 4:6)	(II Tim 4)

I. THE ABSOLUTE NECESSITY OF FAITHFULNESS

I Corinthians 4:17 "For this reason I have sent Timothy to you, who is my beloved and __faithful__ son in the Lord.

I Timothy 3:11; II Timothy 2:2; Proverbs 28:20; Hebrews 3:2; Prov 20:6; Psalm 12:1

A. Defining Faithful

1. One who can be relied on, accountable, steadfast in affection or allegiance, firm in adherence to promises or in observance of duty.

2. One who is a trustworthy person; one who shows himself faithful in business transactions, executions of commands or the discharge of official duties; conscientious, accountable.

B. Synonyms of Faithful

1. Loyal: Implies a firm resistance to any temptation to desert or betray.

2. Constant: Stresses continuing firmness of emotional attachment with strict obedience to promises or vows.

3. Staunch: Suggests fortitude, resolution in adherence and imperviousness to influences that would weaken it.

4. Steadfast: Implies a steady and unwavering course in love, allegiance or conviction.

5. Resolute: Implies firm determination to adhere to a cause or purpose.

6. Commitment: The act of pledging oneself, engaging in a work without thought of quitting or straying off course.

C. God is Faithful and Demands Faithfulness
Deuteronomy 7:9; Isaiah 49:7; Lamentations 3:23; I Corinthians 1:9; 10:13; I Thessalonians 5:24; II Thessalonians 3:3; II Timothy 2:13; Hebrews 10:23; 11:11; I Peter 4:19; I John 1:9

II. THE ABSOLUTE BOTTOM LINE FOR LEADERSHIP = FAITHFULNESS

A. God Chooses Leaders on the Basis of Faithfulness
Matthew 24:45; 25:21-23; Luke 12:42; 19:17; I Timothy 1:12; I Samuel 2:35; 3:20; Nehemiah 9:8; 13:13

B. Godly Men of the New Testament Chose Leaders on the Basis of Faithfulness
I Corinthians 4:17; Ephesians 6:21; Colossians 1:7; 4:7-9; I Peter 5:12; I Timothy 3:11; Titus 1:6

III. THE THREE TESTS OF FAITHFULNESS

A. The Test of Faithfulness in Small Things, *Luke 16:10-13.*

B. The Test of Faithfulness in Another Man's House and Goals, *Luke 16:12; I Corinthians 4:2*

    1. **Moses**, *Exodus 3:1; Numbers 12:7; Hebrews 3:2*

    2. **David**, *I Samuel 16:11; 17:15; 22:14*

C. The Test of Faithfulness in Natural Things, *Luke 16:11; Daniel 6:4; Colossians 3:22; Ephesians 6:6-9*

IV. THE PROGRESS OF A FAITHFUL LEADER

A. Ability — Your Talents, *Matthew 25:15*

B.   Responsibility — Your Delegated Authority, *Mark 13:34*

C.   Accountability — Your Trustworthiness, *Luke 16:2*

D.   Authority — Your Maturity, *Luke 19:7*

"Applying the Truth" Worksheet

1.   Three Insights From This Lesson

       1._____

       2._____

       3._____

2.   What I Need To Work On This Week

_____

_____

_____

_____

3.   Describe the one thing God spoke to you from this lesson.

_____

_____

_____

_____

4.   Other Comments

_____

_____

_____

_____

Timothy Training Program
Session 5: The Choosing, Part I

The Life of Timothy

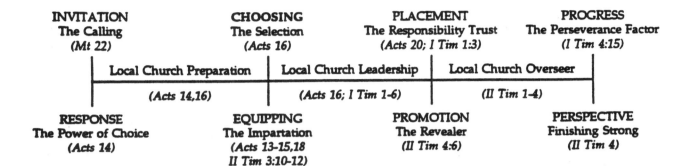

INVITATION The Calling (Mt 22)		CHOOSING The Selection (Acts 16)		PLACEMENT The Responsibility Trust (Acts 20; I Tim 1:3)		PROGRESS The Perseverance Factor (I Tim 4:15)
	Local Church Preparation (Acts 14,16)		Local Church Leadership (Acts 16; I Tim 1-6)		Local Church Overseer (II Tim 1-4)	
RESPONSE The Power of Choice (Acts 14)		EQUIPPING The Impartation (Acts 13-15,18 II Tim 3:10-12)		PROMOTION The Revealer (II Tim 4:6)		PERSPECTIVE Finishing Strong (II Tim 4)

INTRODUCTION: The last several sessions have taken us through the vital steps in preparing the vessel of the Lord. This process develops both the gift and the character of the vessel. We now move on to the area of choosing and equipping. We must bear in mind this is not the initial choosing that takes place prior to preparation. We call that choosing "an invitation." It is an invitation to the Potter's house for the process of becoming a usable vessel of the Lord. The "choosing" we are about to examine is the "selecting for service" that takes place by the Holy Spirit after the gift and character of the vessel have been proven.

I.   **THE CHOOSING,** *Acts 16:3; 13:2*

A. Definition of Chosen

1. Hebrew: To select, choose, pick out

2. Greek: [*ek lego*] To single out, select out from, to prefer

B. The Doctrine of Election, *II Peter 1:10*

    1. Election Definition, *Col 3:12; Titus 1:1; II John 1:13; I Thess 1:4; II Tim 2:10*

        a. Divine selection

        b. To make a choice as from among others

    2. Election According to:

        a. Foreknowledge, *I Peter 1:2*

        b. Grace, *Romans 11:5*

        c. The purpose of God, *Romans 9:11*

        d. Predestination, *Romans 8:29-30*

II. **VESSELS SELECTED BY GOD,** *Acts 15:7; I Chr 7:40; 19:10; Ex 17:9; Ps 65:4; 89:19; Rom 16:13*

    A. Choosing Because of Fruitfulness, *Num 16:7; 17:5; Jn 15:16-19*

    B. Choosing Because of God's Covenant, *Deut 7:6-8*

C. Choosing Because of Character, *Ex 18:20-30*

D. Choosing Because of Courage, *Joshua 8:3*

E. Choosing Because of Changeableness, *I Samuel 17:40*
   (refined by the dealings of God)

F. Choosing Because of Commission, *II Samuel 6:21-22; Deuteronomy 14:2-3; 18:5; 21:5*

   1. Separation to God

   2. Sense of destiny in God

G. Choosing Because of Certainty of Response During Battle, *II Samuel 10:9*

   1. Proven under pressure

   2. Faithful in battle

H. Choosing Because of Commitment to Charge of the Office, *I Chronicles 9:22*

I.   Choosing Because of Cleansing, *I Chronicles 15:15*

J.   Choosing Because of Capacity and Aptitude, *I Chronicles 28:4-6,10; 29:1*

K. Choosing Does Not Guarantee Success, *John 6:70*

L.   Chosen the "Most Unlikely", *I Corinthians 1:27-28; I Samuel 16:7; 11:3*

"Applying the Truth" Worksheet

1. Three Insights From This Lesson

   1._____

   2._____

   3._____

2. What I Need To Work On This Week

   _____

   _____

   _____

   _____

3. Describe the **one** thing God spoke to you from this lesson.

   _____

   _____

   _____

   _____

4. Other Comments

   _____

   _____

   _____

   _____

Timothy Training Program
Session 6: The Choosing, Part II

The Life of Timothy

INVITATION The Calling (Mt 22)		CHOOSING The Selection (Acts 16)		PLACEMENT The Responsibility Trust (Acts 20; I Tim 1:3)		PROGRESS The Perseverance Factor (I Tim 4:15)
	Local Church Preparation (Acts 14,16)		Local Church Leadership (Acts 16; I Tim 1-6)		Local Church Overseer (II Tim 1-4)	
RESPONSE The Power of Choice (Acts 14)		EQUIPPING The Impartation (Acts 13-15,18 II Tim 3:10-12)		PROMOTION The Revealer (II Tim 4:6)		PERSPECTIVE Finishing Strong (II Tim 4)

INTRODUCTION: *Colossians 2:10 (Living Bible) "You have everything when you have Christ."* Whatever purpose God had in placing you on this earth, you have the capacity to accomplish that task. You are equipped to fulfill your call! You have all the potential you need to serve God effectively. You have God's Word, God's Spirit and God's Gift. What are you waiting for?

I. **RECOGNITION OF GIFTING,** *I Timothy 4:14; I Corinthians 12:7*

A. What Are Spiritual Gifts? (refer to special handout on spiritual gifts)

1. Spiritual gifts are special abilities that God gives you to accomplish His work, *I Peter 4:10.*

2. Spiritual gifts are neither identical to natural abilities nor are they totally different. There are both differences and similarities.

a. Only Christians can possess a spiritual gift, *Romans 8:9,14-17; I Corinthians 12:7; 14:16,23-24.*

b. Spiritual gifts are given at the time of spiritual birth, whereas talents come at the time of natural birth.

3. A spiritual gift is a special attribute given by the Holy Spirit to every member of the body of Christ according to God's grace for use within the context of the body.

B. Discover, Develop and Dispense Your Gift, *I Corinthians 12:11,18.*

1. Discover, *I Corinthians 12:7; I Peter 4:10*

    a. Awareness = identifying the spiritual gifts through study and reading

    b. Common Sense = what are your desires, interests.

    c. Confirmation = what do others say about you.

2. Develop

3. Dispense

    a. Move out in faith and obedience

    b. Get involved

II. RECOGNITION OF CHARACTER, *I Timothy 3:1-13; Titus 1:5-9*

A. What is a man of God? How do we recognize a spiritually mature person? When Timothy stayed in Ephesus to help the church mature he came face to face with men who wanted to be teachers and spiritual leaders in the church. In I Timothy 3:1 Paul commanded those who wanted to lead, "It is a fine work he desires, but [he implies] make sure he is a certain kind of man." What Paul says to both Timothy and Titus form a powerful profile for testing a Christian's maturity level. A man of God does not "suddenly appear". He is cultivated in a slow process by the Holy Spirit.

B. Discerning Our Character Maturity

1. Above reproach, *I Timothy 3:2; Titus 1:7*

2. Husband of one wife, *I Timothy 3:2; Titus 1:6*

3. Temperate, *I Timothy 3:2; Titus 1:8*

4. Prudent, *I Timothy 3:2*

5. Respectable, *I Timothy 3:2*

6. Hospitable, *I Timothy 3:2*

7. Able to teach, *I Timothy 3:2*

8. Not given to wine, *I Timothy 3:3; Titus 1:7*

9. Not self-willed, *I Timothy 3:3; Titus 1:7*

10. Not quick-tempered, *I Timothy 3:3; Titus 1:7*

11. Not pugnacious, *I Timothy 3:3*

12. Uncontentious, *I Timothy 3:3*

13. Gentle, *I Timothy 3:3*

14. Free from love of money, *I Timothy 3:3*

15. One who manages his own household well, *I Timothy 3:4; Titus 1:6*

16. A good reputation with those outside the church, *I Timothy 3:7; Titus 1:6*

17. Loves what is good, *Titus 1:8*

18. Just, *Titus 1:8*

19. Devout, *Titus 1:8*

20. Not a new convert, *I Timothy 3:6*

21. Holding fast the faithful word, *Titus 1:9*

C. Character Maturity in the Vernacular

   1. He is a lovable guy!

   2. He is honest. I'd trust him with my bank account.

   3. He is a sensitive person.

4. He radiates Christ.

5. He is a good father.

6. He loves people — his wife, his family, everybody.

7. He works hard.

8. He sure is a humble guy.

9. He keeps his word.

10. He is not self-centered or conceited.

11. He makes you feel comfortable.

12. I can recommend him for most any task.

13. He doesn't let you down.

14. He won't take advantage of you.

15. He is not an opportunist.

16. He doesn't use people for his own ends.

17. He knows where he's going; he plans ahead.

18. He is thoughtful and cordial.

19. He is fair.

20. He is a good steward of time and talent.

21. He doesn't lose his cool.

22. He is consistent.

23. He recognizes and respects authority.

24. He hangs in there and perseveres.

25. He admits when he is wrong.

26. He is teachable.

27. He doesn't have a martyr complex.

28. He is an honest person.

"Applying the Truth" Worksheet

1. **Three Insights From This Lesson**

    1._____

    2._____

    3._____

2. **What I Need To Work On This Week**

    _____

    _____

    _____

    _____

3. **Describe the one thing God spoke to you from this lesson.**

    _____

    _____

    _____

    _____

4. **Other Comments**

    _____

    _____

    _____

    _____

Timothy Training Program
Session 7: The Equipping

The Life of Timothy

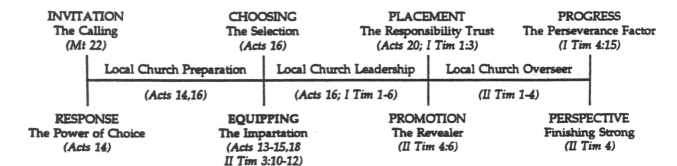

INVITATION
The Calling
(Mt 22)

CHOOSING
The Selection
(Acts 16)

PLACEMENT
The Responsibility Trust
(Acts 20; I Tim 1:3)

PROGRESS
The Perseverance Factor
(I Tim 4:15)

Local Church Preparation
(Acts 14,16)

Local Church Leadership
(Acts 16; I Tim 1-6)

Local Church Overseer
(II Tim 1-4)

RESPONSE
The Power of Choice
(Acts 14)

EQUIPPING
The Impartation
(Acts 13-15,18
II Tim 3:10-12)

PROMOTION
The Revealer
(II Tim 4:6)

PERSPECTIVE
Finishing Strong
(II Tim 4)

INTRODUCTION: We now examine the actual training of Timothy by the Apostle Paul. This stage of preparing a vessel for usefulness is *The Equipping*, which is a very important aspect of training. It is more than teaching. It is training, actually imparting one's life to another. Equipping takes time. To equip means to furnish for service or action, to make ready by appropriate provisioning.

I. RELATIONSHIP: THE FOUNDATION FOR EQUIPPING

A. Paul and Timothy, *II Timothy 2:1*

B. Father/Son Relationship, *Proverbs 1:8,10,15; 2:1; 3:1,11; 4:1,20; 5:1; 6:1; 7:1; 10:1*

II. EQUIPPING OF TIMOTHY, *II Timothy 3:17*

A. His Ministry Experiences

1. Paul's first apostolic journey, *Acts 13:2 - 14:28*

2. Paul's second apostolic journey, *Acts 15:36 - 18:22*

3. Paul's third apostolic journey, *Acts 18:23 - 21:17*

   a. Ephesus Revival, *Acts 19:1-35*

   b. Timothy sent to Macedonia with Erastus, *Acts 19:22*

   c. Timothy sails with team to Miletus, *Acts 20:15,17,18-38*

   d. Timothy stays in Ephesus, *I Timothy 1:3*

B. His Impartation Received From Paul, *II Timothy 3:10-12*

   1. My Doctrine, *Ephesians 4:14; I Timothy 1:3,10; 4:6,13,16*

   2. My Motivation, *Phil 3:13*

   3. My Purpose, *Phil 3:13-14*

   4. My Faith, *I Tim 1:2-5,15,19; 2:7,15; 3:9,13; 4:1,6; 5:8,12; 6:10,12*

5. My Longsuffering, *Eph 4:2*

6. My Love, *I Thess 1:3; Gal 5:6*

7. My Determination, *Phil 3:12-14; II Tim 2:5*

8. My Persecutions with Perspective, *II Tim 3:11; Acts 13:50; 14:5-6,19*

9. My Suffering with Dignity, *II Tim 2:3; 1:8*

"Applying the Truth" Worksheet

1. Three Insights From This Lesson

   1._____

   2._____

   3._____

2. What I Need To Work On This Week

   _____

   _____

   _____

   _____

3. Describe the **one** thing God spoke to you from this lesson.

   _____

   _____

   _____

   _____

4. Other Comments

   _____

   _____

   _____

   _____

Timothy Training Program
Session 8: The Placement

The Life of Timothy

INVITATION The Calling (Mt 22)	CHOOSING The Selection (Acts 16)	PLACEMENT The Responsibility Trust (Acts 20; I Tim 1:3)	PROGRESS The Perseverance Factor (I Tim 4:15)
Local Church Preparation (Acts 14,16)	Local Church Leadership (Acts 16; I Tim 1-6)	Local Church Overseer (II Tim 1-4)	
RESPONSE The Power of Choice (Acts 14)	EQUIPPING The Impartation (Acts 13-15,18 II Tim 3:10-12)	PROMOTION The Revealer (II Tim 4:6)	PERSPECTIVE Finishing Strong (II Tim 4)

INTRODUCTION: Paul has developed Timothy into a strong respected leader through the many trials, teachings and triumphs of their relationship. Paul is now an aged man who is on his way to Rome to be tried and ultimately convicted and beheaded for his faith. Timothy has remained at the great church of Ephesus to give pastoral oversight through his apostolic-type ministry.

I. **EPHESUS: THE CITY, THE CHURCH**

   A. Ephesus: The City

      1. A place of commercial wealth

      2. Temple of Diana was located in Ephesus and was a place of worship as well as a house where treasure was stored

   B. Ephesus: The Church
      Acts 18:18-20; 19:1-6; 19:8-10; 19:11-20; 19:23-41; 20:19-38; Revelation 2:1-7

   C. The Epistle to the Ephesians

II.   THE PLACEMENT OF TIMOTHY AT EPHESUS, *I Timothy 1:3*

   A. Placement with Admonition, *Acts 20:28-32*

      1. To be on guard for yourselves, *Acts 20:28*

      2. To guard the flock as an overseer, *Acts 20:28*

      3. To shepherd the flock, *Acts 20:28*

      4. To fight the savage wolves, *Acts 20:29*

      5. To guard against false leaders, *Acts 20:30*

      6. To be spiritually alert, *Acts 20:31*

      7. To instruct the imbalanced, *I Timothy 1:3*

B. Placement with Perseverance, *I Timothy 1:3*

   1. Prosmeno [Gk] = to cleave to something, remain, continue on in the face of adversity, to take one's station, to anchor.

   2. Spiritual placement means to abide, to stay put, to not let adversity move you, to cleave unto like glue, to determine to remain and bear fruit.

III. **PLACEMENT: PASTORAL CHARGES AND CONCERNS**

   A. Defining Apostolic Charges, *I Timothy 6:13*

      1. Charge [Gk] = *diamarturomai* = to confirm a thing by testimony, cause it to be believed

      2. I Timothy 1:3,18; 5:7,21; 6:13,17; II Timothy 4:1

   B. Twelve Charges Given to Timothy

      1. To keep the teaching pure, *I Timothy 1:3-4,6-7*

      2. To love out of a pure heart and keep a clear conscience, *I Timothy 1:5-6*

      3. To wage war with the prophetic word that went over him *I Timothy 1:18-19*

      4. To continue in fervent prayer, *I Timothy 2:1-8*

      5. To take heed to personal habits and character, *I Tim 4:6; 6:11-13; II Tim 2:22-23*

6. To guard the divine deposit, *I Timothy 6:20; II Timothy 1:12,14*

7. To rekindle the fire of spiritual gifting, *II Timothy 1:6-7*

8. To teach faithful men, *II Timothy 2:2*

9. To be a good soldier, a disciplined athlete and a hard working farmer, *II Timothy 2:3-7*

10. To keep his faith unfeigned, *II Timothy 1:5*

11. To be a qualified minister of the word, *II Timothy 2:15; 4:1-4*

12. A charge concerning the approaching apostasy in the last days, *II Timothy 3:1-9*

IV. CONCLUSION

Timothy was placed at Ephesus as a mighty warrior to guide the church through many spiritual storms. Timothy faced times of discouragement, distress and disappointment but he never gave up his post.

"Applying the Truth" Worksheet

1. Three Insights From This Lesson

   1._____

   2._____

   3._____

2. What I Need To Work On This Week

   _____

   _____

   _____

   _____

3. Describe the one thing God spoke to you from this lesson.

   _____

   _____

   _____

   _____

4. Other Comments

   _____

   _____

   _____

   _____

Timothy Training Program
Session 9: The Promotion

The Life of Timothy

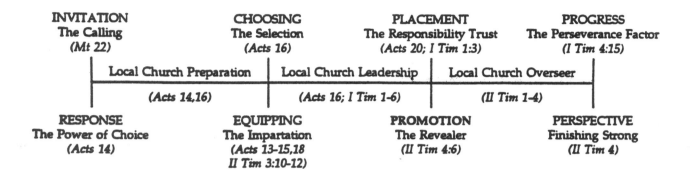

Jeremiah 23:21,32; 27:15; 28:15; 29:9,31; Ezekiel 13:6; Isaiah 55:8-10

PROMOTION: To forward, advance, contribute to growth, enlargement; to exalt, elevate, to raise, to prefer in rank or honor, advancement; to be or become great, high as a mountain, to be blessed, prospered, lifted up.

I.   PURPOSE OF DELAYED PROMOTIONS

A. Spiritual Maturity: the length of time a person can wait between achieving a ministry and being recognized for it.

B. Purpose of Delays

1.   Purifying our motives

2. Trying our inner attitudes

3. Death of a vision

4. Development of one's message

5. Submission of one's will to God's will

6. Demonstrable promotion does not come man's ways

7. Development of true humility

II. WRONG CONCEPTS OF PROMOTION

A. Promotion comes because of what I do not what I am.

B. Promotion comes from the leadership, those over us who are responsible.

C. Promotion comes through taking responsibilities as stepping stones to the top.

D. Promotion comes because of academic training and accomplishment.

E. Promotion comes because of seniority: "I'm the next in line."

F. Promotion comes because of strong inner ambition that drives a person to the top.

III. THE DIVINE PROCESS OF PROMOTION

A. The God Initiative Process
   Psalm 75:4-10; I Samuel 2:1-10; I Peter 5:6; Psalm 132:17; 148:14; Job 36:22; James 4:10

B. Biblical Illustration

   1. Eli — Samuel, *II Samuel 2:3*

   2. Saul — David, *Psalm 92:10; 132:17-18*

3. Righteous — Wicked, *Psalm 75*

4. Esther, *Esther 3:1; 5:11*

5. Shadrach, *Daniel 3:30*

C. Biblical Principles of Promotion

1. Promotion comes when you abide in the place God has set you in, *Judges 9:8-15; I Corinthians 7*

2. Promotion comes when we handle the dealings of God correctly, *Gen 37*

   a. When someone else gets the job you were better qualified for.

   b. When someone seems to belittle your call and talents by ignoring you.

3. Promotion comes when you can rejoice in another person's advancement and serve them, *James 1:9; Matthew 23:11-12*

4. Promotion comes when humility is stronger than self-projection, *Matthew 23:12; I Peter 5:5-6; I Samuel 12:6*

5. Promotion comes when character has been developed and proven to be stable, *Psalm 75:10; 89:16*

6. Promotion comes when there is faithfulness to all jobs given, proving one's love and desire, *Daniel 3:30; Job 36:22-23*

IV. THE AMBITION TRAP

A. Understanding the Word Ambition

1. Dictionary: An eager and sometimes inordinate desire for something, such as preferment, honor, superiority, power, fame, wealth; a desire to distinguish oneself in some way.

2. Greek: laborer for wages; work done for pay and nothing else, no motive for service. It is always used in the New Testament as a fault that ruins a church.

B. End Results of Ambition

1. Self-ambition brings destruction, *Proverbs 17:19*

2. Self-ambition brings shame, *Proverbs 3:35*

3. Self-ambition brings deception, *Obadiah 3-5*

4. Self-ambition causes the body of Christ to come to ruin, *II Corinthians 12:20; 11:26; Galatians 5:20*

5. Self-ambition brings a servant down to abasement, *II Corinthians 10:5; Luke 14:11; 18:14; Ezekiel 21:26*

"Applying the Truth" Worksheet

1.   Three Insights From This Lesson

     1._____

     2._____

     3._____

2.   What I Need To Work On This Week

     _____

     _____

     _____

     _____

3.   Describe the **one** thing God spoke to you from this lesson.

     _____

     _____

     _____

     _____

4.   Other Comments

     _____

     _____

     _____

     _____

Timothy Training Program
Session 10: Progress and Perseverance

The Life of Timothy

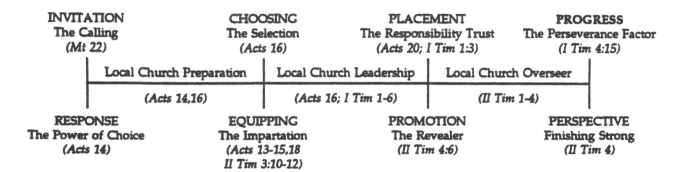

INVITATION The Calling (Mt 22)	CHOOSING The Selection (Acts 16)	PLACEMENT The Responsibility Trust (Acts 20; I Tim 1:3)	PROGRESS The Perseverance Factor (I Tim 4:15)
Local Church Preparation (Acts 14,16)	Local Church Leadership (Acts 16; I Tim 1-6)	Local Church Overseer (II Tim 1-4)	
RESPONSE The Power of Choice (Acts 14)	EQUIPPING The Impartation (Acts 13-15,18 II Tim 3:10-12)	PROMOTION The Revealer (II Tim 4:6)	PERSPECTIVE Finishing Strong (II Tim 4)

II Timothy 4:18; II Timothy 2:1-10; II Peter 1:6

I. DEFINING THE WORD PERSEVERANCE

A. Greek: To remain in a place in spite of opposition; to hold up under; to do something persistently in the face of opposition; to stay one's ground.

B. Dictionary: To pursue steadily any design or course once begun; to be steadfast in purpose; to continue in a given course in spite of difficulties or obstacles; to continue with determination not to give up.

C. Illustrations

1. Thomas Edison conducted some 18,000 experiments before he achieved his goal.
2. Dr. Jonas Salk, who discovered the polio vaccine, worked three long years with many failures before he finally succeeded.
3. Abraham Lincoln failed six times in trying for political office before he became the United States' greatest president.
4. Einstein, considered the greatest genius of the 20th century, said "I think and think for months, for years. 99 times the conclusion is false. The 100th time I am right!"

II.   THREATS TO PERSEVERANCE, *Hebrews 12:1-17*

    A. The Threat of Unconquered Insignificant Sins, *Hebrews 12:1*

    B. The Threat of Undefined Goals and Purposes, *Hebrews 12:1*

    C. The Threat of Deadly Distractions, *Hebrews 12:2*

    D. The Threat of Losing Motivation, *Hebrews 12:2*

    E. The Threat of Becoming Weary, *Hebrews 12:3*

F. The Threat of Wrong Focus, *Hebrews 12:4*

G. The Threat of Reacting Against God-sent Correction, *Hebrews 12:5-11*

H. The Threat of Discouragement, *Hebrews 12:12-13*

I. The Threat of Bitterness that Weakens, *Hebrews 12:15-17*

J. The Threat of Immorality that Steals Our Birthright, *Hebrews 9:16-17*

III. BIBLICAL EXAMPLES OF PERSEVERANCE

A. David, *I Samuel 30:4-10*

B. Shammah, *II Samuel 23:11-12*

C. Paul, *II Timothy 4:7*

D. Job, *James 5:11*

KEEP A-GOIN'

If you strike a thorn or rose,
    Keep a-goin',
If it hails or if it snows,
    Keep a-goin',
Ain't no use to sit and whine,
When the fish ain't on your line;
Bait your hook and keep a-tryin';
    Keep a-goin'.

If the weather kills your crop,
    Keep a-goin',
Though it's work to reach the top,
    Keep a-goin',
Suppose you're out of every dime,
Getting broke ain't any crime;
Tell the world you're feelin' fine,
    Keep a-goin'.

DON'T QUIT!

When things go wrong, as they sometimes will,
When the road you're trudging seems all up hill,
When the funds are low and the debts are high,
And you want to smile but you have to sigh,
    When care is pressing you down a bit,
    Rest, if you must — but don't you quit.

Life is queer with its twists and turns,
As everyone of us sometimes learns,
And many a "failure" turns about
When he might have won if he'd stuck it out;
Don't give up though the pace seems slow,
You may succeed with another blow.

    Often the goal is nearer than
It seems to a faint and faltering man,
Often the struggler has given up,
When he might have captured the victor's cup,
    And he learned too late,
    When the night slipped down,
How close he was to the golden crown.

Success is failure turned inside out —
  The silver tint of the cloud of doubt,
you can never tell how close you are;
It may be near when it seems afar;
So stick to the fight when you're hardest hit —
It's when things seem worse that you mustn't quit.
       —— *Author Unknown*

"Applying the Truth" Worksheet

1. Three Insights From This Lesson

   1._____

   2._____

   3._____

2. What I Need To Work On This Week

   _____

   _____

   _____

   _____

3. Describe the one thing God spoke to you from this lesson.

   _____

   _____

   _____

   _____

4. Other Comments

   _____

   _____

   _____

   _____

Timothy Training Program
Session 11: The Perspective

The Life of Timothy

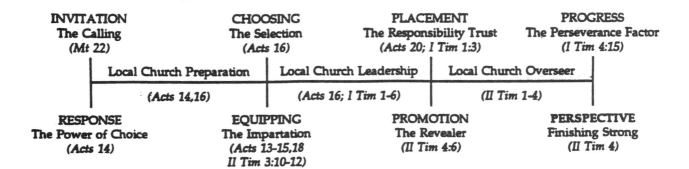

INVITATION	CHOOSING	PLACEMENT	PROGRESS
The Calling	The Selection	The Responsibility Trust	The Perseverance Factor
(Mt 22)	*(Acts 16)*	*(Acts 20; I Tim 1:3)*	*(I Tim 4:15)*
Local Church Preparation	Local Church Leadership	Local Church Overseer	
(Acts 14,16)	*(Acts 16; I Tim 1-6)*	*(II Tim 1-4)*	
RESPONSE	EQUIPPING	PROMOTION	PERSPECTIVE
The Power of Choice	The Impartation	The Revealer	Finishing Strong
(Acts 14)	*(Acts 13-15,18 II Tim 3:10-12)*	*(II Tim 4:6)*	*(II Tim 4)*

I. **THE LEADER'S LIFE AS A DRINK OFFERING**
    Philippians 2:17; II Timothy 4:6; Acts 20:24; Leviticus 6:14; Exodus 29:40-41; II Samuel 23:15

II. **THE LEADER'S OBSTACLE COURSE COMPLETED**
    II Timothy 4:6; I Timothy 6:12; Hebrews 12:1; I Corinthians 9:25-29; Acts 20:24

III. **THE LEADER'S GRIP ON THE FAITH**
    I Timothy 1:19; 2:15; 3:9; 4:1; 5:8; 6:10; 6:12; 6:21; II Timothy 2:18; 3:8

IV. THE LEADER'S PERSPECTIVE ON THE ETERNAL
II Timothy 4:8; Genesis 18:25; I Corinthians 3:13-15

V. THE LEADER'S FORGIVING SPIRIT
II Timothy 4:9-16; II Timothy 4:11-12

VI. THE LEADER'S SECRET OF SUCCESS
II Timothy 4:17-18; II Corinthians 4:7-18; II Corinthians 11:23

A. The Lord Stood With Me

B. The Lord Invigorated Me

C. The Lord Rescued Me

"Applying the Truth" Worksheet

1. Three Insights From This Lesson

   1._____

   2._____

   3._____

2. What I Need To Work On This Week

   _____

   _____

   _____

   _____

3. Describe the one thing God spoke to you from this lesson.

   _____

   _____

   _____

   _____

4. Other Comments

   _____

   _____

   _____

   _____

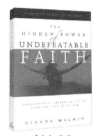
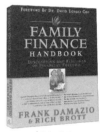